LOST AIRLINE COLOURS OF EUROPE

TIMELINES

First published 2016

Destinworld Publishing Ltd
3 Fairfax Road
Middleton St George
Darlington, Co. Durham DL2 1HF
www.destinworld.com

British Library Cataloguing in Publication Data.
A catalogue record for this book is available from the British Library.

ISBN 978 0 9930950 4 7

CONTENTS

INTRODUCTION

This collection of photographs came about whilst browsing through slides from the 1980s and marvelling at just how many of the airlines and aircraft types have now disappeared from our skies, or changed beyond recognition. A search back into the 1960s and 70s naturally revealed more gems, and even looking forward into the 1990s was a strange experience in realising that so many colour schemes that seemed so run-of-the-mill and common at the time are now a thing of the past.

Thus, this record of some of the most noteworthy airlines and their liveries that have been lost from Europe was collated in the hope that you may also reminisce of trips to airports or flights you have taken in the past.

The nature of the airline industry means that many more will inevitably be added to the lists of lost airlines, and rebranding exercises will see classic schemes disappear. One such example included in this book is that of British Midland Airways, an established airline held in good esteem which itself underwent a significant rebranding in the 2000s, only to disappear completely as recently as 2012.

In other cases you may feel progress has been a good thing. The fussy, awkward liveries common with airlines such as Air France, TAP Air Portugal and Tarom were replaced by stylish, clean and modern schemes which are much better suited.

Opposite Picture:

One of the recent losses from European skies was bmi, or British Midland as it was known to many. Once a dominant force in the British domestic market, and at times an operator of transatlantic charters, European schedules and even Inclusive Tour holiday flights, the airline always wore a variation of blue liveries. This final scheme saw the airline through its final days before it was purchased by the International Airlines Group (IAG), owner of rival British Airways, in 2012.

Aer Lingus

Irish national carrier Aer Lingus adopted this new livery in 1965 with the introduction of its new BAC One Eleven jet aircraft. It featured the now famous shamrock symbol on the tail and a green cheat line along the fuselage.

Aer Lingus took delivery of its first Boeing 737 in 1969 and the type would become the mainstay of its European operations until replaced by Airbus A320 family aircraft in the 2000s. The livery would be replaced by a bolder all-green scheme in the early 1980s, with further alterations in the 1990s.

Aero Lloyd

Aero Lloyd began charter operations with a small fleet of Sud Aviation Caravelle aircraft in 1981, operating from Düsseldorf, Frankfurt and Munich to typical holiday destinations. This early livery was superseded by a brighter variant of the stripes of red and orange when new McDonnell Douglas MD-83 aircraft entered the fleet in the mid-1980s. The airline succumbed to financial pressures and folded in October 2003.

Aeroflot

This unusual picture shows a time of transition for Russian national carrier Aeroflot. Prior to the breakup of the Soviet Union in 1991 Aeroflot aircraft all wore a livery of white fuselage with blue cheat lines and the red Soviet flag on the tail. Here, Ilyushin IL-62 RA-86483 still retains this scheme along its fuselage, but its tail has been painted grey with the new Russian flag.

Air Anglia

With a base at Norwich in East Anglia, Air Anglia was a regional airline and forerunner of Air UK which was formed ten years later. Air Anglia's colourful white, yellow and black livery was found on types such as the Douglas DC-3, Fokker F27 and F28, Embraer Bandeirante, and Handley Page Herald.

Air Atlantis

Portuguese national carrier TAP Air Portugal set up the subsidiary Air Atlantis in 1985 to offer dedicated holiday flights to its resorts, particularly Faro in the Algarve. The airline operated Boeing 707-300, 727-100/200 and Boeing 737-200/300 aircraft on lease from its parent, and featured this scheme not too dissimilar to TAP. The carrier was closed in 1993.

Air Belgium

Air Belgium operated charter flights to leisure destinations using Boeing 737 and 757 aircraft from the early 1980s until 1998 when sold to Airtours. Its aircraft wore this attractive and bright scheme, with OO-ILF seen here. This particular aircraft went on to fly for Britannia Airways and Southwest Airlines.

Air Bridge Carriers / Hunting Cargo

The dedicated cargo airline Air Bridge Carriers was founded in 1972 at East Midlands Airport in the UK. Twenty years later the airline changed its name to Hunting Cargo Airlines, and this picture of Merchantman G-APEP demonstrates the transition period with the red, white and black scheme of Air Bridge with Hunting Cargo titles. Aircraft would later adopt a blue scheme. A sale in 1997 led to the airline changing its name once again to Air Contractors, operating many flights in the livery of DHL.

Air Charter

A charter division of Air France, Air Charter started life as SAFA in 1966 with Sud Aviation Caravelle and Lockheed Super Constellation aircraft from a base at Paris. The Caravelle fleet grew, and in 1969 the airline was renamed Air Charter International, adding Boeing 727-200s in 1972, Airbus A300s and Boeing 737s in 1988. Many of its aircraft were leased from other carriers, including this Caravelle 10B3 from Europe Aero Service wearing the company's final scheme before it was closed down in 1998.

Air Europe

Air Europe was founded in 1979 to offer holiday charter flights from London Gatwick using modern aircraft equipment at a time when the industry was still using aged aircraft and had a reputation for poor quality. The airline was managed by experienced people who had worked in the industry for many years. Its first aircraft were Boeing 737-200s, followed by larger -300 and -400 models, all wearing a bright white, red and orange livery along the fuselage and tail.

Bold ambitions in different markets, such as long-haul schedules and regional connections, an abortive attempts to merge with other airlines eventually wore Air Europe too thin and it closed down in 1991. Interestingly, Air Europa – a Spanish subsidiary wearing a very similar livery – was not owned by the same parent as Air Europe and managed to survive the bankruptcy. It still operates today.

Air France

Air France used variations on the colour scheme seen on this Sud Aviation Caravelle for much of its existence until pioneering the 'Eurowhite' livery in the 1980s that is so familiar of the airline today. This particular

aircraft entered service in 1960 and is seen at London Heathrow in 1976. It spent its entire life flying for Air France.

Air Inter

Early Airbus A300B2 F-BUAH entered service with Air Inter in 1978. This French airline operated domestic scheduled services on trunk routes between major cities and the island of Corsica, with occasional ventures into the holiday charter market before it was merged into Air France in 1997. This scheme which represented the Tricolore flag was worn in various incarnations, starting with that seen on this Caravelle in 1974, and later on the A300 in 1991 shortly before the cheat lines were removed in favour of an all-white fuselage. Air Inter was known for being the only operator of the Dassault Mercure airliner which was developed in France.

Air UK / Air UK Leisure

Air UK was created from the merger of a number of regional airlines in 1980, including Air Anglia, British Island Airways, Air West and Air Wales, in the hope of creating a stronger brand capable of competing on regional routes across the country and into Europe. Its fleet consisted of regional turboprops such as the Fokker F27 (seen here), Handley Page Herald, Embraer Bandeirante and Shorts 360. Early jet types included the BAC One Eleven and later the BAe 146. The airline's early colour scheme consisted of a blue fuselage with red and white cheat lines, and a white tail. Later schemes revised this further before the airline was merged into KLM Cityhopper.

Photo © Paul Schüpbach

In the 1990s Air UK experimented with providing holiday charter flights from a number of British airports using a fleet of Boeing 737-400 aircraft under the Air UK Leisure banner. These wore the same livery as Air UK's other aircraft at the time, with the addition of 'Leisure' titles. In 1993 two Boeing 767-300s were added, and following a sale in 1996 the airline was rebranded Leisure International. It became part of First Choice in 1998.

Airtours International

Photo © Henry Tenby

Emerging as an in-house airline for Airtours Holidays in 1991, Airtours International had a fleet of McDonnell Douglas MD-83 aircraft which were used on holiday charters from the UK. Later Boeing 757-200s were added. When the airline became part of PremiAir in 1996, the livery was changed slightly to include the parent carrier's tail logo. Then, in 2004 the airline was rebranded as MyTravel Airways, taking on a colourful orange and blue scheme. In 2007 the airline was merged into Thomas Cook Airlines.

ATI

Clearly closely tied with Italian national carrier Alitalia, ATI's livery was simply a blue version, including the stylised 'A' on the tail. However, large ATI lettering was included on the forward fuselage. ATI operated many Douglas DC-9s, including N873UM which was formerly I-ATIE but had reverted to the US register briefly. ATI operated domestic schedules and some holiday flights before it was merged into Alitalia in 1994.

Austrian Airlines

Photo © G Zaghini

These colours were for many years the standard at Austrian Airlines, with its fleet of McDonnell Douglas DC-9s and MD-80s seen across Europe on scheduled services. In recent years the carrier has merged with Tyrolean Airways and is now a part of the Lufthansa Group. The present-day livery does offer hints of this classic scheme, but has been modernised.

Aviaco

Aviaco was an independent airline set up to offer domestic links within Spain. It soon started to offer international flights, but was limited in where it could fly due to a monopoly held by Iberia. A real variety of aircraft was operated by the airline, including Bristol 170s, Caravelles, Convair 440s, Fokker F27s, Douglas DC-8s, and from 1974 a large fleet of McDonnell Douglas DC-9s (and later MD-88s). Aviaco was merged into Iberia in 1999.

Aviogenex

Aviogenex was formed as a government subsidiary to operate holiday charters to Yugoslavia from across Europe and its fleet of Boeing 727s, 737s and Tupolev Tu-134s were a common sight at airports across northern Europe. This Boeing 727-200 seen at Manchester in 1996 is wearing the updated livery, based on the original but without the cheat line through the windows and with a cleaner 'AV' logo on the tail.

Balair / CTA

Balair started commercial operations as a charter arm of Swissair, which invested in it. It soon started flying regional scheduled routes, but the addition of long haul aircraft, including this Douglas DC-8-73 led to routes being undertaken to Asia, North and South America from Geneva and Zurich. Balair's livery always reflected that of Swissair, from the white cross on a red tail to the red cheat line along the fuselage.

Compagnie de Transport Aérien, or CTA, was another Swiss regional airline which was founded in 1978. In 1993 it was merged with Balair to create BalairCTA. Following the demise of Swissair in 2001, the company was renamed Belair, which is now part of Air Berlin.

Balkan Bulgarian Airlines

Emerging in 1947 shortly after World War II, Balkan Bulgarian Airlines was built around Soviet transport aircraft, with scheduled links across Europe from its base at Sofia. It was also known for offering holiday charters to Bulgaria's resorts, especially with its Tupolev Tu-154s. This Antonov An-12 was operated as a freighter by the airline. Balkan ceased trading in 2002.

Braathens S.A.F.E.

Photo © Ralf Manteufel

    Braathens South American & Far East Airtransport was founded by Ludvig Braathen in 1946, operating as an independent airline in Norway. It entered the jet age with the delivery of Boeing 737-200 and Fokker F-28 Fellowship aircraft (seen here) in 1969. Its scheme was a common sight at airports across Northern Europe. Prior to the airline's merger with SAS Norway in 2004 it changed to a mostly-white scheme.

Britannia Airways

Formed as Euravia in 1961, this well-known British holiday airline was renamed Britannia Airways in 1964 when Bristol Britannia aircraft were acquired and the Thomson holiday organisation gained control of the airline. Britannia became the first airline in the UK to operate both the Boeing 737 and 767 (seen here), and its aircraft were seen at both summer and winter destinations across Europe, flying from most regional airports in the UK. The airline later became Thomsonfly, and is today known as Thomson Airways.

British European Airways / British Airways

Known as the 'Red Square' livery, British European Airways painted its aircraft in this scheme from the late 1950s, featuring a black and white fuselage with red squares framing white BEA titles both on the tail and behind the cockpit. Its fleet at the time comprised many piston and turboprop types, and the livery lasted for the introduction of jet airliners such as the de Havilland Comet 4, Hawker Siddeley Trident and BAC One Eleven.

From the late 1960s BEA started painting its aircraft in the new 'Speedjack' livery, featuring a Union Jack on the tail and green cheat line along a white and grey fuselage. Following the merger of BEA and BOAC to create British Airways in 1974, many of the aircraft retained this livery as an interim measure until they could be painted in the new Landor scheme.

British Airways was formed in 1974 from the merger of BOAC and British European Airways, creating one national, government-owned carrier to operate services across Europe and around the world. It called for a new branding and livery which lasted until 1984 when this new scheme was introduced by Landor Associates, adding a touch of sophistication. It is seen here on BAC One Eleven G-AWYS at Birmingham in 1994. Note that at this time some aircraft operating from regional bases as Birmingham and Manchester had additional titles added. The Landor scheme would last until the controversial world tail schemes and new branding were introduced in 1997, followed by the present Union Flag livery became standard from 2001.

BEA Airtours

BEA Airtours was founded as a charter and holiday flight arm of British European Airways in 1969. With the merger of BEA and BOAC in 1974 it became known as British Airtours. Here, Boeing 707 G-ARWD

demonstrates the first livery, which is an adaptation of the BEA "Speedjack" scheme worn at the time.

British Caledonian

One of the most lamented airlines from the United Kingdom, British Caledonian started life when Caledonian Airways merged with British United Airways in 1970, creating the largest independent airline in the country, and offering serious competition to the government owned national airlines, which were soon to merge to form British Airways. British Caledonian played on its Scottish heritage, but was focussed on services out of London to destinations across Europe and in Africa and North America. It used a mixed fleet of aircraft types both large and small, from the Vickers Viscount to the Boeing 747. BAC One Eleven G-ASJC shows the blue, gold and white scheme with golden lion on a blue tail fin as it taxies at London Gatwick in 1975.

A network of feeder flights were offered into London Gatwick with added 'Commuter' titles. Vickers Viscounts were used on the service, and later the regional airline Genair was pressed into action to feed BCal's hub using its Embraer Bandeirante, Short 330 and 360 aircraft. This was the first commuter network of its kind in the UK, and emulated that developed by Allegheny Airlines in the USA.

British Caledonian entered a tough period of trading in the 1980s and was ultimately merged with its greatest rival, British Airways in 1988.

Photo © Peter Frei

British Island Airways

British Island Airways, or BIA, existed in two different periods. It first operated for nine years between 1971 and 1980 when it was merged into the newly formed Air UK and operated aircraft such as the Douglas DC-3, BAC One Eleven and Handley Page Herald on short-haul scheduled passenger and freight services, particularly to the Channel Islands. In 1982 the airline was bought back, commencing services with BAC One Elevens and McDonnell Douglas MD-83s before it ceased trading in 1991.

British Midland Airways

British Midland Airways was the new name for Derby Aviation, which had formed in 1938 but by 1964 sought something more universal. Vickers Viscount aircraft like this one were a common sight on its UK domestic services out of London Heathrow and its home base at East Midlands.

British Midland adopted this royal blue scheme in the mid-1980s, a time when in addition to its McDonnell Douglas DC-9 jet fleet, it also operated Shorts 360s and British Aerospace ATPs (seen here) on various domestic routes. The airline would later acquire Boeing 737s, Fokker 70/100s, and Airbus A320 family aircraft, with a name change to bmi, before it was ultimately acquired by British Airways' parent, IAG, in 2012.

British United Airways

British United Airways became a major regional airline in the UK during the 1960s, with bases at London Gatwick and Stansted airports, and a significant cross-channel operation to France and the Channel Islands. This Vickers Viscount shows the airline's original livery, consisting of a dark blue cheatline with a smaller gold stripe, and the Union Jack flag on an otherwise white tail. Later British United would adopt a green and white scheme as it took on more aircraft and grew in size.

British Air Ferries

Photo © Peter F Peyer

British Air Ferries was the new name for British United Air Ferries, a subsidiary of British United Airways. It started life as a car ferry service between the UK and France operating Carvair aircraft, and would go on to operate Handley Page Heralds and a significant fleet of Vickers Viscounts before being put into receivership in 1993.

British World Airlines

The assets of British Air Ferries were purchased and turned into British World Airlines, operating some of the Viscounts in freighter capacity, and a

fleet of BAC One Eleven, BAe 146 and Boeing 737s on charter work. It too entered receivership in December 2001.

Brymon Airways

Resting between flights, this Handley Page Herald shows off the colourful yellow and blue scheme worn by Brymon Airways. Although it did operate jet aircraft in the form of BAC One Elevens, Brymon focused largely on an all-turboprop fleet including de Havilland Canada's DHC-6, DHC-7 and DHC-8. The airline became British Airways Citiexpress in 2002.

Caledonian Airways

Caledonian Airways had been a famous name in the British airline industry, growing out of Scotland and eventually becoming British Caledonian (BCal). British Airways resurrected the name following its merger with Bcal by rebranding its British Airtours charter arm in 1988 and using the famous lion motif on the tail. The airline took on a darker livery, with gold stripe on a near black underbelly. Caledonian's fleet comprised mainly Lockheed TriStar and Boeing 757-200 aircraft, plus McDonnell Douglas DC-10, Airbus A320 and Boeing 737-200s. In 1989 this sole Boeing 747-200 was operated on long-haul charters.

Channel Airways

When Southend-based Channel Airways bought second-hand Viscount aircraft from Continental Airlines in the United States, they came wearing their former owner's livery. Channel decided to save money by adopting this as their own livery, with only minor changes, and even retained the Continental Golden Jet titles on its jet aircraft. The Hawker Siddeley Trident

From the collection of the late John Woods

was not a major success and few were sold. The first independent airline to buy a Trident was Channel Airways which used it on holiday charters in an impressive seven-abreast seating arrangement.

Conair

This Danish charter airline commenced operations in 1965 using a fleet of Douglas DC-7 aircraft in a basic white scheme with red cheatlines and stylised tail logo showing the letter 'C' around a red sun. By the time the jet age arrived, first with Boeing 720s and later Airbus A300s, the airline adopted a livery with different shades of blue, still retaining the same tail logo. Conair merged with Scanair in 1993 to form PremiAir, which is now Thomas Cook Airlines Scandinavia.

Court Line

Photo © Ralf Manteufel

These two pictures demonstrate one of the most memorable liveries seen in the 1970s. British airline Autair was rebranded as Court Line in 1970 as it took on jet aircraft in the form of BAC One Elevens and a pair of brand new Lockheed L1011 TriStars. Each aircraft in the fleet wore a different shade of pastel colours, demonstrated here on both of the L1011s seen at Berlin in June 1973.

Photo © Ralf Manteufel

Crossair

Crossair was formed to connect cities around Europe with Swiss hubs in Basel, Geneva and Zurich. Cooperation with Swissair aligned the operations of the two carriers, feeding in to long haul flights in particular. Crossair operated a variety of regional aircraft, including the SAAB 340 and 2000, and the Avro RJ. Seen here in 1997 is RJ100 HB-IXU wearing the airline's last livery (still including the cross of the Swiss flag on the tail as worn by all international airlines from the country) before the demise of Swissair in 2001. Crossair would later be rebranded

CSA Czechoslovak Airlines

Known affectionately by enthusiasts and passengers as the 'OK Jet', CSA Czechoslovak Airlines was another Eastern European carrier influenced by Soviet aircraft designs. It operated Ilyushin IL-18s and IL-62s, Tupolev Tu-134s and Yakovlev Yak-40s. Following the break up of Czechoslovakia the airline remained the flag carrier of the Czech Republic and retained the CSA name, but has rebranded and now operates modern Airbus aircraft.

Cyprus Airways

Only a recent loss to the aviation world, Cyprus Airways operated from 1947 until 2015. During the 1980s it expanded into the holiday market, flying its Boeing 707s and 720s across Europe before modern Airbus A310s were acquired. These joined a small fleet of BAC One Elevens operating regional schedules. The orange and blue scheme made way for a smarter blue scheme, and was changed again in the 1990s and 2000s, with the final scheme seen here on Airbus A320 5B-DBC. All variations of the livery featured the stylised fly mouflon flying goat on the tail.

Dan-Air London

Reflecting the dominance of Dan-Air London in the 1970s, this scene shows many of the carriers aircraft sat at London Gatwick awaiting their next assignments. The airline was noted for having a mixed bag of aircraft types, including the world's largest fleet of Comet 4Bs, and BAC One Elevens, both seen here. Also visible are two Boeing 707s of British Airtours.

Familiar to anyone who flew on holiday flights and European schedules in the 1970s and 80s, Dan Air London was a fiercely independent airline which made its own path, acquiring a mixed bag of aircraft types and a real mix of operations, with bases at London Gatwick and Manchester. It was the first British airline to operate the Boeing 727, with an early - 100 variant seen here.

Donaldson International Airways

The Bristol Britannia was chosen as the workhorse for the new Donaldson International Airways in 1968, allowing it to undertake charter work from bases at Glasgow and London Gatwick airports. By 1972 these aircraft had been replaced by Boeing 707s which could carry either passengers or cargo. However the airline was short-lived and ceased trading in 1974.

Estonian Air

Estonian Air was quickly established following the break-up of the Soviet Union in 1991, when Estonia and neighbouring countries all gained independence. The airline initially operated various Soviet-built airliners before turning to Western equipment such as the Boeing 737 and Fokker 50. From 2011 modern regional jets such as the Embraer 170 and Bombardier CRJ900 (seen here) started joining the fleet to operate regional routes. The smart livery featured different tones of blue on white running along the fuselage.

Estonian Air ceased operations in 2015 when it was determined that government funding received by the airline was illegal and must be paid back.

First Choice Airways

During the 2000s the British holiday and charter airline industry underwent many changes and consolidations. Airlines that had become quite established were suddenly rebranded or merged with other carriers and new identities formed. In the case of Air 2000, an airline formed in 1987, it was rebranded First Choice Airways in 2004 to reflect the name of the parent company. Leisure International had already been acquired in 1998, bringing Boeing 767-300 aircraft to the fleet, as seen here. The livery used was essentially that of the holiday company parent.

In 2008 First Choice Holidays merged with TUI AG and its Thomsonfly airline to create Thomson Airways, a descendent of Britannia Airways (see earlier).

Hapag-Lloyd

The airline arm of the Hapag Lloyd Shipping Group commenced flights to holiday destinations from various West German airports in 1972. It began operations with Boeing 727s, 737s BAC One Elevens and Airbus A300s that wore this livery matching that of the parent shipping company and its thousands of containers seen in ports around the world. Later model 737s, such as the -400 and this -500 were introduced in the 1990s, alongside Airbus A310s. By the 2000s next generation 737-800s joined the fleet, and the carrier was sold to TUI AG in 2007, rebranded as HapagFly with a number of its aircraft leased by the new low-cost carrier Hapag-Lloyd Express. Today it is part of the TUIfly brand.

Hispania Líneas Aéreas

Hispania was a holiday charter airline based in Palma de Mallorca and founded in 1983 to capitalise on the growing tourism market from northern Europe to Spain's resorts. Its first aircraft were four Caravelle

10Rs. EC-CYI is seen at Manchester in 1984 awaiting trolley-loads of bags and still wearing the carrier's original livery which would be updated before its demise in 1989.

Iberia

Photo © Clint Groves/Air Transport Photography

Throughout the 1960s and 70s Iberia, the national carrier of Spain, painted its aircraft in this livery which was similar to many other European airlines at the time. A globe with the letters IB and a Spanish flag adorned the white tail. Iberia established a new livery in the 1980s across its fleet which played further on the colours of its national flag and IB lettering, and has only recently been replaced by a modern 'Eurowhite' scheme. The Boeing 727-200, seen here at London Heathrow in 1975, was the backbone of Iberia's European and domestic routes.

Inter European Airways

Commencing services with a Boeing 737-200 in 1987, Inter European Airways had a complicated typeface and colourful livery representative of its charter work to sunny destinations. Boeing 737-300s and -400s, as well as 757-200s and Airbus A320s were operated from UK airports before the airline was merged into Airtours International.

Interflug

When Germany was still divided the national carrier of the German Democratic Republic of East Germany was Interflug. The state-owned carrier provided scheduled services, holiday charters, government and military flying and many other aviation activities. It was known for operating a fleet of Soviet airliners, including this Tupolev Tu-134 which by the time of the photograph in 1990s is wearing its new unified German registration of D-AOBD. Interflug was closed down a year later.

Invicta Airways

This British charter airline flew a real mix of early piston and turboprop aircraft types, including the Vickers Vanguard, and even the Boeing 707. Its work mostly consisted of short cargo and passenger flights to Europe. Vanguard G-AXOO, seen here in 1971, flew with the airline from 1970 until it was scrapped in 1977.

Istanbul Airlines

Seen at Düsseldorf in 1989 on one of its key tourist charter routes, TC-AKA was a Caravelle 10R which flew for Turkish carrier Istanbul Airlines on holiday charter flights bringing tourists to holiday destination. It underwent a number of changes to its livery and operated various different jet aircraft types before ceasing operations in 2000.

Itavia

Photo © Gianluigi Parpani

A troubled Italian airline plagued with operational difficulties and a high profile crash of one of its McDonnell Douglas DC-9 aircraft, Itavia existed from 1958 until 1981 when it gave way to ATI on domestic scheduled services. Here N94454 is at Milan Linate airport in 1989, retaining its US registration whilst on lease from Hawaiian Airlines.

JAT

Jugoslovenski Aerotransport, or JAT, was the national airline of Yugoslavia. From 1947 it operated as a scheduled passenger airline linking Yugoslav cities with the rest of Europe. It acquired jet aircraft in the 1970s, including this McDonnell Douglas DC-9-32, YU-AHN, plus Boeing 707s, 727s and. 737-300s. A McDonnell Douglas DC-10-30 was also used on transatlantic schedules. Following the break-up of Yugoslavia the airline resumed flying as Jat Airways, based in Belgrade. It was recently rebranded Air Serbia.

Jersey European

Anyone familiar with the UK domestic airline Flybe may wonder why it uses the call sign 'Jersey'. It is in fact a descendent of Jersey European - itself formed out of the merger between two other small airlines in 1979. Jersey European was based on the Channel Island of Jersey and flew a network of domestic routes across the UK and international services to France. The orange livery seen here on Fokker F27 G-JEAB was replaced by a mostly white scheme in the 1990s, shortly before the airline was rebranded British European. Then in 2002 it was renamed again as Flybe.

KLM Royal Dutch Airlines

The world's oldest airline, KLM, dates back to 1919. Today we're familiar with the all-over shades of blue which adorns its large fleet of aircraft and those of its Cityhopper subsidiary. Here in 1968 one of its Douglas DC-9s is docked at an air bridge at Amsterdam Schiphol wearing the previous

incarnation, with bands of two different shades of blue across the tail and down the fuselage. A white top and metal bottom finish off the scheme, which was worn across KLMs fleet until the early 1980s. On some aircraft the banding on the tail would be diagonal rather than horizontal.

LTU / LTU Süd

LTU and its subsidiary LTU Süd built up a large presence in Germany. Formed in 1955 it flew short-haul charter and scheduled services with piston aircraft such as the Vickers Viking. During the 1980s LTU became a big player in the holiday charter market, offering flights from hubs such as Düsseldorf and Frankfurt to destinations throughout southern Europe. LTU Süd was formed in 1984 to operate Boeing 757s out of Munich. LTU was one of the few European airlines to fly the wide-body Lockheed TriStar. Today LTU is owned by Air Berlin and all aircraft wear this livery.

Lufthansa

Lufthansa became the world's first operator of the Boeing 737. An example of the rare -100 model is seen here at Manchester in the 1970s wearing the colour scheme that lasted until the 1980s, but which is not too dissimilar to that worn today. The blue cheatline, black nose cone and metal-finish underbelly were replaced with an all-white fuselage and larger titles, yet the yellow crane emblem on a blue tail were retained.

Maersk Air

Photo © Max Fankhauser

    Like Hapag Lloyd in Germany, Maersk Air was founded as an arm of a giant shipping line, based in Copenhagen, Denmark. Its aircraft wore a distinctive light-blue scheme. Turboprop aircraft such as the DHC-7, Fokker F27 and this F-50 were employed on regional scheduled services, whilst the airline also flew Boeing 720 and 737-200/300 aircraft on holiday charters. Maersk was bought by Sterling Airlines in 2005.

MALEV Hungarian Airlines

A recent shock departure from the skies of Europe was Hungarian national airline MALEV which succumbed to years of financial pressure and ceased flying in February 2012. Another Eastern Bloc carrier which favoured Soviet-built airliners, types such as the Tupolev Tu-134 and Tu-154 seen here soldiered on with the airline into the 1990s even as western types were being added.

Manx Airlines

The red, white and green livery worn by Manx Airlines' aircraft were always notable for the symbol of three legs joined together worn on the tail. The airline name and this symbol are identifiers of the people of the Isle of

Man, between Britain and Ireland, from where this regional airline hailed. It operated turboprop and some jet equipment between 1982 and 2002. This BAe ATP joined the fleet in 1994.

Monarch Airlines

One of Britain's longest serving leisure airlines. Monarch has endured many changes in the industry and fought on through the inclusive tour holiday market of the 1970s and 80s, the low cost boom of the 1990s and 2000s, and is today a purely scheduled airline offering affordable flights to holiday destinations from a select number of UK bases. In its early days Monarch's fleet replaced Bristol Britannia aircraft with BAC One Elevens and Boeing 737s, with G-DFUB seen on a ski charter to Geneva in 1986. Monarch was also an early adopter of the Boeing 757-200, and Britain's only operator of the Airbus A300B4-600 variant. The livery based around bright yellow has always been a part of Monarch's image and is still a feature today.

NLM CityHopper

Few airports in the United Kingdom and northern Europe are without feeder services by KLM Cityhopper today. However, this carrier has its routes in an early feeder operation known as NLM CityHopper, founded in 1966 to operate domestic flights within the Netherlands on behalf of its parent, KLM. Fokker F28 jet aircraft joined the F27s in 1978, and international destinations were added. The carrier was renamed KLM Cityhopper in 1991.

Northeast Airlines

Northeast Airlines was the new name of BKS Airlines, a carrier which operated largely from northern England and London Heathrow. Becoming part of the British Air Services group, Northeast took on a bold livery of yellow, grey and white, which was very modern and stylistic in the early 1970s. The airline was named because it mainly operated out of Newcastle and Teesside airports in North East England. Its Tridents and Viscounts operated a mix of scheduled and charter services, but the airline would be consumed by the creation of British Airways in 1974, with aircraft briefly wearing the new carrier's titles over the yellow scheme until all were repainted fully.

Olympic Airlines

Arguably one of the most memorable liveries to have come from Europe, Olympic Airlines was the national carrier of Greece between 1957 and 2009 after an extended period struggling with losses. The livery employed by the airline changed in subtle ways throughout its existence, but retained the iconic coloured rings on a blue tail consistently from 1959 until its demise. Because the International Olympic Committee claimed copyright on the five-ringed logo, a sixth ring was added by the airline as a solution.

Orion Airways

Orion Airways was the airline arm of Horizon Holidays, a UK travel firm offering inclusive tour charters to the sun. The airline's livery of browns, yellows and oranges may look garish today, but were seen as bright and

sunshine-like in the 1980s. Orion operated a large fleet of Boeing 737-200 and -300 aircraft, and two Airbus A300B4s (as seen here) bought from Lufthansa for use on high-density leisure routes.

Ryanair

Ryanair has become one of the largest and most significant airlines in Europe in recent years, with a giant fleet of Boeing 737NG aircraft flying on hundreds of routes. However, the airline had more humble beginnings as a regional airline offering scheduled flights between Ireland, the UK and Europe. Its early fleet included Embraer Bandeirante, ATR 42 and BAC One Eleven aircraft in a basic, mostly white livery, as seen on EI-BSY at Birmingham in 1988. The airline would change beyond recognition in the 1990s as it transitioned into a "no frills" low cost carrier.

Sabena

Belgian national carrier Sabena was founded in 1923 to connect Brussels with cities around the world, and particularly focusing on colonies in Africa. This Boeing 707 is seen landing at London Heathrow in the 1970s wearing the early blue scheme with smaller titles than used on later liveries.

One of the many liveries worn by Sabena in its long life before it ceased flying in 2001. This 'Eurowhite' scheme still incorporated the stylised 'S' logo on the tail, but had more subtle titles along the fuselage. Note also the stickers denoting the airline's collaboration with Swissair. Both airlines would be early casualties following the September 11, 2001 terrorist attacks and the subsequent downturn in aviation felt around the world.

SAS Scandinavian Airlines System

Scandinavian Airlines System, or SAS, was created in 1946 by merging the national airlines of Denmark, Norway and Sweden, with the route networks of all three being merged across the three countries. Douglas DC-8-33s such as this example were retired from the airline by 1971, however this early livery continued until the 1980s.

From the 1980s SAS painted its aircraft in this mostly white livery featuring a band of colours under the forward fuselage which comprised the flags of Denmark, Norway and Sweden. The flags also appeared on the engines. SAS was famous as a Douglas DC-9 and later McDonnell Douglas MD-80 series operator, flying the types throughout Europe until Boeing 737 and Airbus A320 variants took over during the early 2000s. This livery was replaced at a similar time.

Sobelair

This Belgian airline operated as the charter arm of national carrier Sabena for much of its existence. Sobelair was founded in 1946 and acquired by its new parent in 1949. Many of its aircraft were leased from, or purchased second-hand from Sabena, and wore a very similar livery including the same 'S' tail logo. Following the demise of Sabena in 2001, Sobelair was retained by new national carrier SN Brussels Airlines in 2003, but closed down in January 2004.

Spanair

A familiar sight at airports across Europe until 2012, Spanair was a Spanish charter and scheduled airline. Founded in 1986 to offer holiday flights, it developed a network of scheduled services both within Spain and to other European cities, joining the Star Alliance in 2003. Spanair operated a large fleet of McDonnell Douglas MD-80 series aircraft throughout its existence, along with Boeing 767-300s for long haul services. Later, Airbus A320 family aircraft joined the fleet.

Spantax

This page shows two variations of the colour scheme worn by one of Spain's best remembered charter airlines. Formed in 1959 to ferry oil workers in Africa and operating piston airliners, the lure of the new holiday market to Spain soon came calling. In 1967 the first jet airliners were acquired in the form of two Convair 990s. These were later joined by a mixed bag of Douglas DC-8s, McDonnell Douglas DC-9s and DC-10s, and Boeing 737-200s. The larger aircraft operated long-haul charters and high density routes, whilst the smaller types could be found plying their trade across northern Europe and on various domestic routes. The airline ceased trading during a difficult financial period in 1988.

Sterling Airways

Copenhagen-based Sterling Airways was a holiday charter airline founded in 1962. It acquired a fleet of jet airliners, including Douglas DC-8s, Caravelle 10Bs (seen here) and Boeing 727-200s. OY-STD is seen here at Rimini awaiting passengers for its return journey in 1990, with 'Sky Jets' titles applied to the engines and forward fuselage.

Swissair

Swissair's simple and easily recognisable livery of the 1980s saw cheat lines of brown and black, with the white cross on a red tail familiar of many Swiss carriers. This would be updated to a mostly white fuselage in the 1990s before Swissair became victim to the global downturn in aviation in 2001. It was relaunched as Swiss International Air Lines.

TAE

Trabajos Aereos y Enlaces, commonly known as TAE, was a Spanish charter airline flying tourists to resorts in the country, in particular to its home base of Palma de Mallorca. It operated BAC One Elevens, Douglas DC-7s, DC-8s and Sud Aviation Caravelles at different times during its brief career, which lasted from 1967 to 1981. Caravelle 10B3 EC-CUM joined the fleet in 1976 and shows clearly the airline's red and white scheme with stylised aircraft logo on the tail.

TAP Air Portugal

This early livery with titles explaining the meaning of 'TAP', namely Transportes Aereas Portugueses, is demonstrated on Sud Caravelle CS-TCC in 1975. Today the airline is known universally as TAP Portugal with a much brighter scheme. This particular aircraft went on to fly in Ecuador.

Tarom

Tarom has been the national carrier of Romania since 1954 when it replaced the pre-war airline LARES. This early colour scheme of red cheat lines and bird logo, with the country's flag on the tail, is seen on Ilyushin IL-18 YR-IMF, which operated for the airline between 1964 and 1997. The livery would be modified in the 1970s to include the bird logo on the tail,

before the present-day blue livery was adopted in the 1990s. For a while Tarom was associated with ROMBAC One Elevens, built locally under license from the UK. The airline was interested in that it operated a mix of Soviet and Western types alongside each other for many years.

TAT European Airlines

Photo © Ralf Manteufel

TAT European Airlines was founded as Touraine Air Transport in 1968 to operate domestic and air taxi flights within France. Originally its aircraft wore a bright mostly yellow scheme. However, in the 1990s this modern variation was adopted with bold TAT titles in blue. Following purchase by British Airways in the late 1990s, TAT was eventually merged with Air Liberté and AOM.

TEA Trans European Airways

Trans European Airways, or TEA, was formed in 1970 as a leisure operator to carry holidaymakers from Belgium to various Mediterranean destinations. It commenced operations with a Boeing 720 and later acquired an Airbus A300B1 and numerous Boeing 737-200s. The airline's livery features large blue TEA lettering and tail. The European flag was incorporated into the tail in the 1990s. Various subsidiaries were formed in Italy, the UK and Switzerland. Seen here is a TEA Swiss Boeing 737-300 wearing its red variation of the livery. TEA Swiss would later become easyJet Switzerland.

Photo © R Shaw

THY Turkish Airlines

The pinstripe colours of Türk Hava Yollari, or THY, were seen across Europe and further afield in the 1970s and 1980s. This Boeing 727-200 was one of eight flown by the carrier, alongside Airbus A310s, McDonnell Douglas DC-9s and DC-10s, Boeing 707s and Fokker F27s. From the

1990s the airline became universally known as Turkish Airlines and now has one of the world's largest fleets of Boeing 737NG and Airbus A320 family aircraft, alongside long-haul 777s and Airbus A330/40s.

Transavia Holland

Always envisaged as a charter airline, Transavia Holland was formed in 1965 with Douglas DC-6 equipment. Later it flew Sud Aviation Caravelles and Boeing 707s, and briefly Airbus A300s and Boeing 757s. However, from the 1980s it has always focused on the Boeing 737, from the classic -200 and -300 models (seen here at Corfu), to today's Next Generation -700 and -800 models.

Tyrolean Airways

Tyrolean was a regional airline based in Innsbruck, Austria, operating regional scheduled services across Europe. Its fleet consisted of regional turboprops and jets, such as this Fokker 70, all painted in an attractive red, yellow and white livery. Tyrolean provided connecting flights on behalf of Austrian Airlines, who acquired the carrier in 1998. It was rebranded Austrian Arrows in 2003 before becoming wholly incorporated into the parent airline in 2012.

UTA Union de Transports Aeriens

Union de Transports Aeriens (UTA) became a major French airline during its brief existence. Formed out of a merger between two smaller carriers in 1963, it took on a global presence linking all corners of the globe, and particularly French territories. Later its large widebody aircraft wore a bold blue tail with unusual green doors on a white fuselage. Its first livery, seen here on Caravelle 10R F-BNRB in 1967, was more modest.

Viva Air

Vuelos Internacionales de Vacaciones, or Viva Air for short, was a bright and colourful airline established as a partnership between Iberia and Lufthansa to capitalise on the booming holiday market from northern Europe to Spain and is coastal and island resorts in the 1990s. Viva Air's livery was a simple design created by school children which represented the sunshine and holiday spirit to be found in Spain. The airline operated a number of Boeing 737-300 and McDonnell Douglas DC-9-32 aircraft and even ventured into scheduled flying, until it was closed in 1999.

ABOUT THE AUTHOR

Matt Falcus has had a lifelong interest in aviation. He is the author of a number of books on aircraft and airports, and has written for magazines such as Airliner World, Airports of the World and Aviation News. He is the editor of AirportSpotting.com

Also by the Author

Handley Page Herald Timelines
ISBN: 978-0-9930950-1-6

The Herald was an innovative British airliner which started life as a piston aircraft and had to be quickly reimagined to utilise turboprop engines in order to keep up with the competition. This book tells the story of the Herald from its inception through to its entry into service, the airlines that operated it, and the remaining examples today.

World Airports Spotting Guides
978-0-9930950-3-0

Detailed spotting guides to over 300 worldwide airports. Find out exactly where to watch aircraft, where to take photographs, and what kind of aircraft you'll see there. Includes spotting hotels, museums and other attractions.

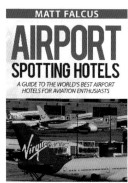

Airport Spotting Hotels
ISBN: 978-0-9930950-6-1

Make the most of every trip by finding a room at an airport hotel with a view. Airport Spotting Hotels details over 270 hotels in 54 countries that offer views of aircraft movements, including details of the best rooms and what you'll see.

COULD YOU WRITE A *TIMELINES* BOOK?

Authors with specialist subjects are being sought to bring it to life as a *Timelines* book.

Timelines seeks to tell the story of a subject from its earliest days to the present day, or looking at a particular period in time. The series, which relies heavily on photographic and archive images, covers local history, transport, sport and social history. Any subject will be considered.

Get in touch today with your idea by visiting **www.destinworld.com** or sending an email to **info@destinworld.com**